# 11+
## English
### Success

Age 6–7
Age 7–8
Age 8–9
Age 9–10
Age 10–11

**Assessment Papers**

**How to succeed in the 11+ tests**

Alison Head

# Sample page

level showing attainment target

paper number for quick reference

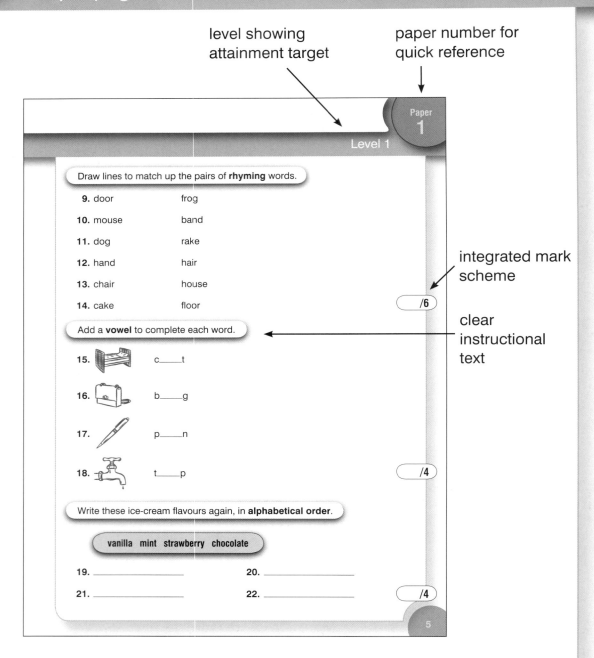

integrated mark scheme

clear instructional text

# Contents

| | |
|---|---|
| PAPER 1 | 4 |
| PAPER 2 | 7 |
| PAPER 3 | 9 |
| PAPER 4 | 12 |
| PAPER 5 | 14 |
| PAPER 6 | 17 |
| PAPER 7 | 19 |
| PAPER 8 | 22 |
| PAPER 9 | 24 |
| PAPER 10 | 26 |
| PAPER 11 | 28 |
| PAPER 12 | 31 |
| PAPER 13 | 34 |
| PAPER 14 | 36 |
| PAPER 15 | 38 |
| PAPER 16 | 41 |
| PAPER 17 | 44 |
| PAPER 18 | 46 |
| PAPER 19 | 49 |
| PAPER 20 | 52 |
| PAPER 21 | 54 |
| PAPER 22 | 57 |
| PAPER 23 | 60 |
| PAPER 24 | 62 |
| Glossary | 65 |
| Progress grid | 67 |
| Answer booklet | 1–4 |

**Paper 1 — Level 1**

## PAPER 1

We saw crazy creatures at the zoo
Tiny tree frogs, green and blue
Stripy tigers with strong, sharp jaws
Lion cubs with big soft paws
An elephant with a wavy trunk
An anteater and a smelly skunk.

But the creature crazier than any other
Was my funny little brother!

**Circle your answers.**

1. Where did the children see the animals?

    at school          (at the zoo)          on a farm

2. Which was the craziest creature?

    tree frog          elephant          (little brother)

**Answer these questions.**

3. Find and write down a word from the poem that rhymes with 'jaws'.

    _paws_

4–5. Write down two colours that are mentioned in the poem.

    _green_          _blue_

6. Find and write down a word from the poem that means "small". _Tiny_

7. Which animal in the poem has stripes? _tigers_

8. Write a sentence saying which of the animals in the poem you would most like to see, and why.

    _Tiny tree frogs because I have not seen one._

8 /8

Paper 1

Level 1

Draw lines to match up the pairs of **rhyming** words.

9. door      frog
10. mouse    band
11. dog      rake
12. hand     hair
13. chair    house
14. cake     floor

6 /6

Add a **vowel** to complete each word.

15.    c_o_t

16.    b_a_g

17.    p_e_n

18.    t_a_p

4 /4

Write these ice-cream flavours again, in **alphabetical order**.

vanilla   mint   strawberry   chocolate

19. ___chocolate___      20. ___mint___
21. ___strawberry___     22. ___vanilla___

4 /4

5

**Paper 1**

## Level 1

> Write each sentence again, adding a **question mark**.

**23.** Where is the playground

_Where is the playground ?_

**24.** Who is playing with Mark

_Who is playing with Mark ?_

**25.** How many kittens are there

_How many kittens are there ?_

**26.** What is your name

_What is your name ?_

/4

> Write a word that begins with each of these blends.

**27.** bl_aze_

**28.** cr_ab_

**29.** tr_ain_

**30.** str_aw_

/4

/30

# PAPER 2

Here comes Kate. She is on her way to the sweet shop to buy some chocolate. Kate loves chocolate more than anything. She buys some every Friday. Today, she is going to buy a new type of chocolate bar. It has little bits of fudge in it. Kate will love the shiny pink wrapper. She loves pink almost as much as she loves chocolate!

Circle your answers.

1. What is the name of the girl in the story?

   (Kate)　　　　　　　　Clare　　　　　　　　Sarah

2. On what day each week does she buy chocolate?

   Tuesday　　　　　　　Sunday　　　　　　　(Friday)

Answer these questions.

3. What does the new type of chocolate have in it? __bits of fudge__

4. What colour does Kate like? __pink__

Invent a new chocolate bar of your own. Draw it in the box.

5. What is the name of your chocolate bar?

   __sweety choc__

On your drawing, label these things.

6. The shape of your chocolate bar. __rectangle__

7. The main colour of the wrapper. __pink__

8. The colour of the writing on the wrapper. __blue__

/8

# Paper 2

## Level 1

**9–16.**

Sort these letters into **vowels** and **consonants**.

| b | e | o | c | t |
|---|---|---|---|---|
|   | i | m | u |   |

| vowels | consonants |
|--------|------------|
| e | b |
| o | c |
| i | t |
| u | m |

8 /8

Write the **plural** for each word.

17. car _____cars_____  18. ball _____balls_____

19. room _____rooms_____  20. school _____schools_____

21. game _____games_____  22. picture _____pictures_____

6 /6

Write these sentences again, with a capital letter at the beginning.

23. the party was great fun.

The party was great fun.

24. my brother is called Martin.

My brothe is called martin.

25. it is too wet to play outside.

It is too wet to play outside.

26. we went to the zoo at the weekend.

We went to the zoo at the weekend.

4 /4

8

# Paper 3

## Level 1

Write the two words that each **compound word** is made from.

27. handbag — hand — bag
28. toothbrush — tooth — brush
29. footpath — foot — path
30. eyebrow — eye — brow

4/4

30/30

## PAPER 3

**That's rubbish!**

We throw a lot of rubbish away. Some of it can be collected and used to make new things, like glass bottles or recycled paper. Some of it can be used to make compost, to help our plants grow. Other rubbish cannot be used again. It is often buried in the ground or burned to make energy. If we put all of our rubbish in the right bin, we will be able to use as much as possible to make new things.

It is never right to drop litter. It looks messy and can be dangerous for wild animals.

Answer these questions.

1. What does the text say compost can be used for?
   to help plants grow.

2–3. List two things that often happen to rubbish that can't be used again.
   buried — burned

**Paper 3**

## Level 1

**4.** What do you think the word *recycled* means?

*New thing.*

*When you turn something into something.*

**5–6.** Find two reasons why it is never right to drop litter.

*It looks messy*     *dangerous for animals.*

**7.** What does the text say we should do with our rubbish?

*put in right bin.*

**8.** Write a sentence about what you do with your rubbish at home. Is some of it collected to make other things?

*I recycble by making something out of trash.*

**8 /8**

Sort the words with the same letter patterns into the boxes.

**9–14.**

| toy | cow | towel |
|-----|-----|-------|
| hard | royal | car |

| **ow** words | **ar** words | **oy** words |
|--------------|--------------|--------------|
| *row* | *hard* | *toy* |
| *towel* | *car* | *royal* |

**5 /6**

10

Paper 3

Level 1

Complete the word for each picture.

15.  tr_ee_   16.  b_oa_t

17.  b_oo_k   18.  tr_ai_n

19.  m_oo_n   20.  r_oa_d

6 /6

Complete these word sums.

21. look + ing = __looking__        22. walk + ed = __walked__

23. wait + ing = __waiting__        24. follow + ed = __followed__

25. sing + ing = __singing__         26. talk + ed = __talked__

6 /6

Write these sentences again, adding the capital letters.

27. it was cold when i woke up.

__It was cold when I woke up.__

28. my best friend is called chris.

__My best freind is called Chris.__

29. we went to london on the train.

__We went to london on the train.__

30. my party is on friday.

__My party is on friday.__

4 /4

29 /30

11

# PAPER 4

**Level 2**

**The lion and the mouse**

One day a mighty lion caught a tiny mouse.

"Please do not eat me," said the mouse. "Let me go, and one day I promise to help you in return."

The lion laughed. "You are tiny and I am big and strong. How could you ever help me? However, I can see that you are brave, so I will let you go."

Some time later, some hunters caught the lion in a net. They were going to send him to a circus, far away. The lion roared and struggled but the more he wriggled, the more tangled he became in the net. He was strong, but not strong enough to break the net.

Suddenly, the little mouse appeared and began to chew through the net. Soon the lion was free.

"Thank you my friend," said the lion. "I set you free and now you have freed me. You may be tiny, but you have the bravery of a lion!"

**Circle your answers.**

1. Which word is used in the first sentence to describe the size of the mouse?

    small          (tiny)          thin

2. What does the mouse think the lion will do to him?

    rescue him          (eat him)          play with him

**Answer these questions.**

3. Why does the lion decide to set the mouse free?

    Because the mouse was brave.

4. Who catches the lion? _____ hunter _____

5. What do they want to do to the lion? take to circus

Paper 4

Level 2

**6–7.** Find and copy two words that describe how the lion moved in the net.

_staggered_   _wriggled_

**8.** Do you think a mouse would make a good meal for a lion? Give a reason for your answer.

_NO, because to the mouse is not enought for the lion._   8/8

Add **wh** or **ch** to complete each word.

9. _ch_ air
10. _wh_ ere
11. _wh_ en
12. wat_ch_
13. _wh_ y
14. _ch_ ain

6/6

Draw lines to match up the pairs of **antonyms**.

15. huge — tiny
16. buy — sell
17. lose — find
18. high — low
19. inside — outside
20. fast — slow

6/6

Underline four of the **time** words in this piece of text.

**21–24.** We had great fun at the cinema. While Dad bought the tickets, Mum bought popcorn and during the film we shared it. When the film had finished, we went to the restaurant next door for pizza. Afterwards, we went home.

3/4

13

# Paper 5

## Level 2

Underline the correct **verb** in the brackets to complete each sentence.

25. I (am are) the tallest in my class.
26. My friends (is are) coming to tea.
27. Our dog (play plays) with her favourite ball.
28. The teacher (writes write) on the whiteboard.
29. Mum (are is) angry when my bedroom is untidy.
30. Children (is are) not allowed in the staff room at school.

6/6

29/30

## PAPER 5

When twins Maisie and Molly are sent to stay with their great-aunt for the summer, mysterious things start to happen. What is in the locked room at the end of the landing? Where does Great Aunt Maud go each night? And can Oscar the cat really talk?

The twins soon realise that this summer will be anything but boring!

Answer these questions.

1. This is the **blurb** from the back of a book. What is a "blurb" for?

   To summrise the book.

Paper 5

Level 2

**2.** Does the blurb make you want to read this book? Give a reason for your answer.
_Yes, beccause it is really intresting_

**3.** Find a word in the blurb that means the same as "strange" or "odd".
_mysterious_

**4.** What do you think might be in the locked room? _guns_

**5.** Invent a title for the book. _Mysterous stories_

**6–7.** Design a cover for the book below. Label the title and add another label to explain why you have chosen the picture.

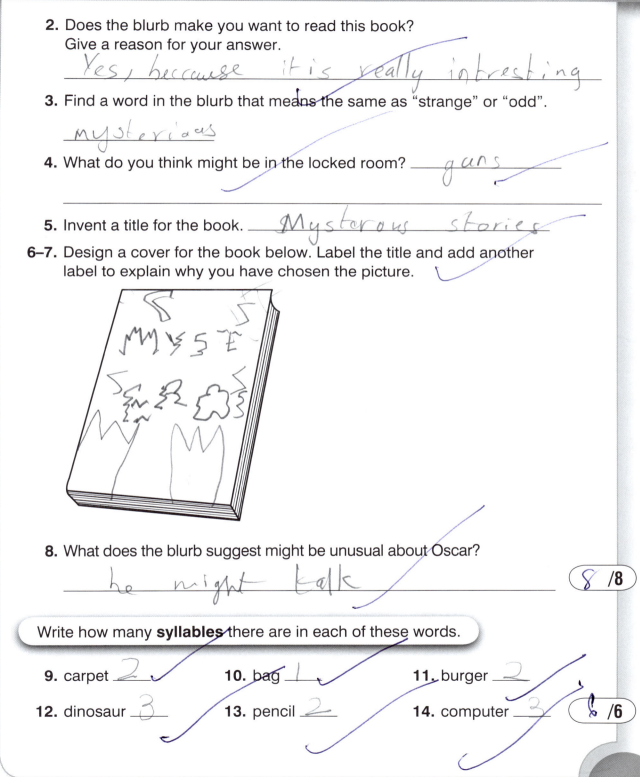

**8.** What does the blurb suggest might be unusual about Oscar?
_he might talk_

8 /8

Write how many **syllables** there are in each of these words.

**9.** carpet _2_    **10.** bag _1_    **11.** burger _2_

**12.** dinosaur _3_    **13.** pencil _2_    **14.** computer _3_

6 /6

15

# Paper 5

## Level 2

> Underline the words in each sentence that have been spoken by a character.

**15.** "Go away!" shouted the man, crossly.

**16.** The bear asked, "Who has been sitting in my chair?"

**17.** "Look out for the ladder!" warned Dad.

**18.** Sally giggled, "You have chocolate all round your mouth!"

/4

> Draw lines to join the pairs of words with similar meanings.

**19.** rush      smashed     **20.** walk     large

**21.** unhappy     hurry      **22.** huge      hot

**23.** broken      sad      **24.** warm     stroll

/6

> Add a **comma** to each sentence.

**25.** My school uniform is blue, grey and white.

**26.** Last night we had pizza, pasta and salad for tea.

**27.** My friends are called, Tom, Max and Paul.

**28.** You can play football, tennis and basketball at the park.

/4

> Write two interesting sentences about what you can see from your bedroom window:

**29.** Outside are cars and buses

**30.** roads.

/2

26/30

Paper 6

Level 2

## PAPER 6

**Chocolate crispy cakes**

You will need:
150 g of milk chocolate
100 g crisped rice cereal
12 paper cake cases

1. Break the chocolate into chunks and place in a heat-proof bowl.
2. Ask an adult to boil a little water in a saucepan. Turn off the heat.
3. Place the bowl on top of the saucepan, taking care not to let the bottom of the bowl touch the water.
4. Stir the chocolate as it melts.
5. Add the crisped rice cereal and stir carefully until the cereal is coated in chocolate.
6. Place a spoonful of the mixture into each cake case.
7. Place in a fridge to set.

Circle your answers.

**1.** How much chocolate do you need to make the cakes?

100 g          (150 g)          250 g

**2.** How many cakes will you make?

6          (12)          20

Answer these questions.

**3.** Why should you ask an adult to boil the water? *harm you*

*Because you could get burned*

**4.** How do you know when to stop stirring the chocolate and cereal mixture?

*When it is melted.*

**5.** Why do you put the cakes in the fridge? *Harded*

# Paper 6

## Level 2

*Intro to make food*

6. This text is a recipe. What does the word *recipe* mean?

   how to cook something.

   /6

Add the **suffixes** to complete each word sum.

7. slow + ly = slowly    8. joy + ful = joyful
9. play + ful = playful  10. kind + ly = kindly
11. bad + ly = badly     12. tear + ful = tearful

   6/6

Choose the best question word from the brackets to complete each sentence.

13. Who ___ is your favourite teacher? (When  Who)
14. when ___ will tea be ready? (Where  When)
15. where ___ did you leave your bag? (Where  Who)
16. why ___ are you late? (Where  Why)

   4/4

Write a sentence using each of these **adjectives**.

17. huge

    The huge cake blasted in the kitchen

18. gentle

    The dog gentely picked up the ball

19. shiny

    I had a shiny bell.

20. spooky

    It was a spoocky night

   /4

Level 2

Paper 7

Underline the silent letter in each word.

**21.** knife
**22.** gnome
**23.** calm
**24.** scissors
**25.** stalk
**26.** sign

6 /6

Draw lines to match each word with its **definition**.

**27.** pavement — the liquid inside many fruits

**28.** school — two weeks

**29.** fortnight — a place where children go to learn

**30.** juice — a footpath that runs alongside a road

4 /4

30 /30

## PAPER 7

The beautiful queen walked elegantly into the room with her head held high. Her long silk gown swished as she walked and jewels jangled lightly at her ears and around her neck. The scent of her rose perfume filled the room.

Answer these questions.

**1–2.** Find and copy two words that describe sounds.

_swished_    _jangled_

**3.** What smell is mentioned in the description? _rose_

# Paper 7

## Level 2

Now imagine a wicked fairy. Use the boxes to jot down words or phrases you could use to describe her.

| | |
|---|---|
| **4.** Words and phrases that describe how she looks<br><br>ugly<br><br>pig like | **5.** Words and phrases that describe how she moves<br><br>wierdly |
| **6.** Words and phrases that describe how she smells<br><br>yukkty    old shoes<br><br>rotten eggs | **7.** Words and phrases that describe how she sounds<br><br>crocked |

**8.** Use your ideas to write a short description of the wicked fairy.

Maybe Later.?

/8

Add *le* to complete each word.

**9.** cand_le_    **10.** bubb_le_    **11.** tab_le_

**12.** midd_le_    **13.** crad_le_    **14.** circ_le_

/6

20

Paper 7

Level 2

Underline the **prefix** in each word.

**15.** disabled      **16.** react      **17.** unhappy

**18.** defrost      **19.** preschool      **20.** review

/6

Write each sentence again using a word from the brackets instead of the word "said".

**21.** "You are so naughty!" said the teacher crossly. (snapped giggled)

"You are so naughty!" ~~sp~~ snapped the teacher crossly.

**22.** "Can I have a drink please?" said Kate. (replied asked)

"Can I have a drink please? ~~sa~~ asked Kate.

**23.** "Be careful near the water," said Mum. (warned wondered)

"Be careful near the water", warned Mum

**24.** "Don't wake the baby," said Dad. (whispered shouted)

"Don't wake the baby" ~~so~~ whispered Dad.

/4

Draw lines to match up the pairs of **verbs** with similar meanings.

**25.** jump      yell

**26.** eat      creep

**27.** sleep      gobble

**28.** shout      scrub

**29.** tiptoe      doze

**30.** clean      leap

/4

/30

21

# Paper 8

### Level 2

## PAPER 8

By the time the train pulled into the station, it had started to rain. We lifted our heavy cases onto the platform and carried them into the warm, dry waiting room. Our summer holidays always began in that waiting room. Grandma would promise to meet us off the train but something would always hold her up. Someone would telephone about a sick cow, or bring in an injured cat, and she would stay behind to see what she could do. Grandma was the only vet for miles around and she could not stand to see animals suffer.

**Circle your answers.**

1. What is the weather like in the story?

   it is sunny    (it is rainy)    it is windy

2. What season does the story take place in?

   (summer)    autumn    spring

3. What job does the children's Grandma do?

   train driver    farmer    (vet)

**Answer these questions.**

4. Where do the children go to shelter from the rain?

   _____waiting____room_____

5–6. Find and write down the names of two animals mentioned in the story.

   _____cow_____    _____cat_____    /6

**Underline the verb in each sentence.**

7. Our dog sleeps on my bed.    8. Marco loves pizza.

9. Dad read the boys a story.    10. Lara lost her book.

11. Ali won the art competition.    12. The woman drove the car too quickly.

/6

Paper 8

Level 2

Circle the **compound word** in each pair.

13. eggshell    jelly            14. turtle       wallpaper
15. station     playground       16. armchair     blanket
17. seaside     picture          18. cushion      teaspoon

/6

19–22. Label these instructions a–d to put them in the correct order.

**Crossing the road safely**

d  When it is safe, walk straight across the road without running.

a  Choose a safe place where you can see the road clearly in both directions.

c  Look left and right and wait until there is no traffic in either direction.

b  Stand a little way back from the kerb.

Complete these word sums.

23. small + er = _smaller_        24. tall + est = _tallest_
25. fast + est = _fastest_        26. old + er = _older_
27. loud + est = _loudest_        28. kind + er = _kinder_
29. slow + est = _slowest_        30. quiet + er = _quieter_

/8

/30

## Paper 9

### Level 2

## PAPER 9

**Fox Wood comes first!**

Fox Wood Primary School is celebrating this week after winning first prize in a national gardening competition for schools. The school beat around 200 others to win the competition, which involved planning and planting a vegetable garden.

Gardening club member Julie Smith, aged 8, explains: "Our playground is round so we decided to match it with a circular garden, with lettuce and tomatoes on one side and peas and beans on the other. They have grown really fast and we are very proud of our garden."

The school has won a new greenhouse and six sets of child-sized gardening tools. The members of the gardening club will also be special guests at the West Midlands Flower Show later this month.

**Circle your answers.**

1. How many schools took part in the competition?

   (around 200)          around 300          around 250

2. How old is Julie Smith?

   7          (8)          9

3. What shape was Fox Wood's vegetable garden?

   square          (circular)          triangular

**Answer these questions.**

4. Why did the gardening club choose this shape for their garden?

   _because play ground is round_

5–6. Find and write down two of the things the club grew in their vegetable garden.

   _peers_          _beans_

**Paper 9**

**Level 2**

**7.** What word does Julie use to describe how the club feels about their garden?

_Proaund_

**8.** The club wins a greenhouse. What is a *greenhouse*?

_a place to grow plants._

/8

> Write the two words that have been joined together in each **contraction**.

**9.** don't  ___do___  ___not___

**10.** I'm  ___I___  ___am___

**11.** he'll  ___He___  ___will___

**12.** we're  ___we'___  ___are___

**13.** they've  ___they___  ___have___

**14.** couldn't  ___could___  ___not___  /6

> Add the silent letter to each word.

**15.** _k_nee  **16.** fo_r_k

**17.** thum_b_  **18.** s_il_ent

**19.** desi_g_n  **20.** cou_l_d  /6

**21–26.** Add two words of each type to the table.

| noun | verb | adjective |
|---|---|---|
| Ridha | ran | happy |
| Dsg | jump | sad |

/6

25

# Paper 10

## Level 2

**27–30.** Write four sentences describing your bedroom. Include information about its size, the colour of the walls and your favourite things.

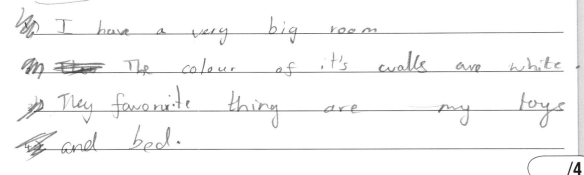

/4

/30

## PAPER 10

10th November

Dear Auntie Margaret,

Thank you for offering to take care of Scamp while we are on holiday. We will drop him off next Saturday morning on the way to the airport. I will pack up his bed, food bowls, food and lead, so you should have everything that you need.

We normally take Scamp for a walk twice a day, before his breakfast in the morning and again in the afternoon. He is usually quite good but he does like to chase rabbits so it might be a good idea to keep him on his lead in the woods!

Thanks again. See you next Saturday,

Philip x x x

Circle your answers.

1. Who wrote this letter?

   Auntie Margaret        Scamp        (Philip)

**Paper 10**

**Level 2**

**2.** What type of animal do you think Scamp is?

(a dog)  a cat  a rabbit

**3.** How will Philip's family reach their holiday destination?

by train  (by aeroplane)  by ferry

> Answer these questions.

**4.** What is the letter thanking Auntie Margaret for?

To take care of the dog.

**5–6.** Find and write down two things that Philip will pack for Scamp.

food  lead.

**7.** What does Philip suggest Scamp might do in the woods?

chase rabbits

**8.** How does he suggest Auntie Margaret could stop this from happening?

keep him on lead.

/8

> Write these words again in alphabetical order.

**scrap  storm  slipper  snore  smile  save**

**9.** save

**10.** scarp

**11.** slipper

**12.** smile

**13.** snore

**14.** storm

/6

> Change the **vowel** in the middle of each word to make another word.

**15.** cut  cot

**16.** mop  map

**17.** man  men

**18.** pin  pan

**19.** ten  tan

**20.** bet  bat

/6

27

## Level 2

Add a **question mark** or **exclamation mark** to each sentence.

**21.** Is it going to rain later ?

**22.** Where is the park ?

**23.** Your dress is amazing !

**24.** You must be joking !

**25.** Who is at the door ?

**26.** Go away !

/6

Circle a word in each group that has more than one meaning.

**27.** train     (path)     horse

**28.** desk     (fair)     ribbon

**29.** (wall)     left     teacher

**30.** ticket     shoe     (light)

/4

/30

## PAPER 11

### GUMBO'S CIRCUS

Gumbo's fantastic circus is coming to Hedley Green for one week only.

- Be amazed by Marco the fire-eater
- Marvel as the Tito twins cross the tightrope with no safety net
- Laugh as Coco the colourful clown takes to the ring

Tickets are on sale now. Book quickly to avoid disappointment!

Buy 2 adult tickets and get one child ticket completely free!

Level 2

### Circle your answers.

**1.** What is the poster advertising?

(a circus)    a funfair    a theatre

**2.** What is the name of the fire-eater?

Mark    Martin    (Marco)

**3.** What is Coco?

an acrobat    (a clown)    a magician

### Answer these questions.

**4.** What do the Tito twins not use in their act? _saftey net_

**5.** What special offer is available if you buy tickets? _buy 2 adult ticket_
get _one child ticeet free._

**6.** Which of the three acts on the poster would you most like to see? Give a reason for your answer.

_fire eater because it is a very hard trice._

/6

### Add *ph* or *f* to complete each word.

**7.** tele_ph_one

**8.** _f_ish

**9.** _f_unny

**10.** gra_pe_

**11.** _ph_ysical

**12.** _f_aster

/6

**13–16.** Circle the words you could add the **prefix *un*** to, to make opposites.

(friendly)    slip    (happy)    (careful)

(helpful)    young    (sure)

/4

# Paper 11

## Level 2

> Write a sentence using each **verb/adverb** pair.

**17.** crept silently

*The witch crept silently behind the girl*

**18.** laughed happily

*The couple laughed happily.*

**19.** shouted angrily

*The teacher shouted angrily at the naughty kid.*

/3

> Draw lines to match up the pairs of **present tense** and **past tense verbs**.

**20.** run — came

**21.** bring — went

**22.** come — wrote

**23.** write — ran

**24.** read — brought

**25.** go — read

/6

**26–30.** Add at least five sentences to this story opening. Remember to use capital letters and full stops.

### A surprise for Mr Peel

One day, an unusual parcel arrived at Mr Peel's pet shop. Inside was a large, pale blue egg. Mr Peel had never seen anything like it. He left the egg in a warm place to see if it would hatch.

30

A few days later, Mr Peel noticed that the egg had cracked. It was hatching! Mr Peel peered closely to see what was inside.

A ~~some~~ small little eye peak~~ing~~ed at him as innocent as an angle. He could not belive it... it... it was a DRAGON! A ~~big~~ baby dragon.

/5

/30

## PAPER 12

**Digby gets ready to ride!**

Merton Peaks Theme Park opens for the summer season this Saturday with a brand new ride designed especially for young visitors. The Digby Dipper is an exciting new roller-coaster for children under 10 years old. The ride has a dinosaur theme and the track winds through a prehistoric landscape complete with models of dinosaurs including Digby, who gives his name to the attraction.

Park manager Eve Lawrence explains: "We wanted a central character that both boys and girls would like. We thought a friendly dinosaur would be ideal. Digby won't be scaring anyone but his ride is pretty fast and very high, so there will be plenty of thrills!"

Digby is offering one lucky reader and a friend the chance to be the first to try the new ride. Just write a letter to Digby explaining why you should be the first to try his ride. Good luck!

# Paper 12

## Level 2

**Circle your answers.**

**1.** When does Merton Peaks open for its summer season?

next week　　　　(this Saturday)　　　　next month

**2.** What age group is the ride designed for?

(under 10 years)　　　over 10 years　　　adults

**Answer these questions.**

**3.** Why did the theme park choose a dinosaur as the character for the new ride?

_____because girls and boys like it_____

**4–5.** Find two reasons why the park manager says the ride is quite scary.

_____high_____　　_____fast._____

**6–8.** Add at least three sentences to complete this letter to Digby.

Digby Dinosaur
Merton Peaks Theme Park
Merton
Derbyshire

Dear Digby,

I think my friend (your friend's name) _____ and I should be the first people on your new ride because

_____We are not easy to scary_____
_____and love roller coasters too._____
_____&_____
_____._____

Thank you for reading my letter,

_____Ridha_____ (your name)

/8

Paper 12
Level 2

Circle the correct word in the brackets to complete each **collective noun**.

9. a ((flock) bunch) of sheep
10. a (fleet (herd)) of cows
11. a (hand (bunch)) of grapes
12. a ((pack) pick) of cards

/4

Underline the **adjective** in each sentence.

13. Dad made us a <u>delicious</u> picnic.
14. The sea was <u>calm</u>.
15. I am reading an <u>interesting</u> book.
16. Auntie Karen bought me some <u>blue</u> sandals.

4

Write the **plural** of each word.

17. house — houses
18. pencil — pencils
19. train — trains
20. book — books
21. banana — bananas
22. chair — chairs

/6

Add the correct **consonants** to complete a label for each picture.

23. b_ea_r
24. p_ea_ch
25. ea_r
26. p_ea_rs

/4

Write down **antonyms** for these words.

27. big — small
28. awake — ~~std~~ sleeping
29. off — on
30. old — new

/4

/30

33

# Paper 13

## Level 2

## PAPER 13

Dear Diary,

What a day it has been! It all began this morning when the washing machine leaked all over the kitchen floor. There was water and bubbles everywhere! Then Dad came in from painting the garden fence and slipped on the wet floor. He skidded across the kitchen with the paint pot in his hands then dumped the whole lot onto the hall carpet.

Mum tried to clear up the paint but the more she scrubbed at it, the bigger the stain got!

The water has been cleared up now, but the kitchen floor and the hall carpet are ruined. It's a good thing we are off to Spain on Wednesday. Uncle Tom says he will get them replaced while we are away. I hope tomorrow is calmer!

**Circle your answers.**

1. What leaked all over the kitchen floor?

   paint          (the washing machine)          the kitchen sink

2. What had Dad been painting?

   the hallway          the house          (the garden fence)

3. Where is the family going on holiday?

   Spain          (France)          Italy

**Answer these questions.**

4. Find and copy a word with a similar meaning to *slipped*.

   _slid_

5. What happened when Mum tried to clear up the paint?

   the stain got bigger

# Answer booklet: Assessment English age 7–8 years

## Paper 1
1. at the zoo
2. little brother
3. paws
4–5. green, blue
6. tiny/little
7. tiger
8. Answers will vary.
9. floor
10. house
11. frog
12. band
13. hair
14. rake
15. cot
16. bag
17. pen
18. tap
19–22. chocolate, mint, strawberry, vanilla
23. Where is the playground?
24. Who is playing with Mark?
25. How many kittens are there?
26. What is your name?
Answers might include:
27. black
28. creep
29. train
30. street

## Paper 2
1. Kate
2. Friday
3. fudge
4. pink
5–8. Answers will vary.
9–16. Vowels: e, o, i, u
Consonants: b, c, t, m
17. cars
18. balls
19. rooms
20. schools
21. games
22. pictures
23. The party was great fun.
24. My brother is called Martin.
25. It is too wet to play outside.
26. We went to the zoo at the weekend.
27. hand      bag
28. tooth      brush
29. foot      path
30. eye      brow

## Paper 3
1. helping plants grow
2–3. buried in the ground; burned to make energy
4. used to make new things
5–6. it looks messy; it can be harmful to wildlife
7. put it in the right bin
8. Answers will vary.
9–14. *ow* words: cow, towel
*ar* words: hard, car
*oy* words: toy, royal

15. tree
16. boat
17. book
18. train
19. moon
20. road
21. looking
22. walked
23. waiting
24. followed
25. singing
26. talked
27. It was cold when I woke up.
28. My best friend is called Chris.
29. We went to London on the train.
30. My party is on Friday.

## Paper 4
1. tiny
2. eat him
3. because he thinks he is brave
4. hunters
5. send him to a circus far away
6–7. struggled, wriggled
8. Answers will vary.
9. chair
10. where
11. when
12. watch
13. why
14. chain
15. tiny
16. sell
17. find
18. low
19. outside
20. slow
21–24.
We had great fun at the cinema. While Dad bought the tickets, Mum bought popcorn and during the film we shared it. When the film had finished, we went to the restaurant next door for pizza. Afterwards, we went home.
25. am
26. are
27. plays
28. writes
29. is
30. are

## Paper 5
1. A blurb tells people what the book is about.
2. Answers will vary.
3. mysterious
4. Answers will vary.
5. Answers will vary.
6–7. Answers will vary.
8. that he can talk
9. 2
10. 1
11. 2
12. 3
13. 2
14. 3
15. "Go away!" shouted the man, crossly.

16. The bear asked, "Who has been sitting in my chair?"
17. "Look out for the ladder!" warned Dad.
18. Sally giggled, "You have chocolate all round your mouth!"
19. hurry
20. stroll
21. sad
22. large
23. smashed
24. hot
25. My school uniform is blue, grey and white.
26. Last night we had pizza, pasta and salad for tea.
27. My friends are called Tom, Max and Paul.
28. You can play football, tennis and basketball at the park.
29–30. Answers will vary.

## Paper 6
1. 150 g
2. 12
3. Because boiling water could harm you.
4. When the rice cereal is coated in melted chocolate.
5. So that the melted chocolate will set.
6. Instructions for making food.
7. slowly
8. joyful
9. playful
10. kindly
11. badly
12. tearful
13. Who
14. When
15. Where
16. Why
Answers will vary but may include:
17. A huge cake sat in the window of the bakery.
18. The mother cat was gentle with the kittens.
19. Magpies like to collect shiny things.
20. The empty old house was spooky.
21. knife
22. gnome
23. calm
24. scissors
25. stalk
26. sign
27. a footpath that runs alongside a road

28. a place where children go to learn
29. two weeks
30. the liquid inside many fruits

## Paper 7
1–2. swished, jangled
3. rose perfume
4–8. Answers will vary.
9. candle
10. bubble
11. table
12. middle
13. cradle
14. circle
15. <u>dis</u>abled
16. <u>re</u>act
17. <u>un</u>happy
18. <u>de</u>frost
19. <u>pre</u>school
20. <u>re</u>view
21. snapped ("You are so naughty!" snapped the teacher crossly.)
22. asked ("Can I have a drink please?" asked Kate.)
23. warned ("Be careful near the water," warned Mum.)
24. whispered ("Don't wake the baby," whispered Dad.)
25. leap
26. gobble
27. doze
28. yell
29. creep
30. scrub

## Paper 8
1. it is rainy
2. summer
3. vet
4. waiting room
5–6. cow, cat
7. sleeps
8. loves
9. read
10. lost
11. won
12. drove
13. eggshell
14. wallpaper
15. playground
16. armchair
17. seaside
18. teaspoon
19–22. d, a, c, b
23. smaller
24. tallest
25. fastest
26. older
27. loudest
28. kinder
29. slowest
30. quieter

## Paper 9
1. around 200
2. 8
3. circular
4. to match their circular playground
5–6. any two of: lettuce, tomatoes, peas, beans
7. proud
8. a small building made of clear glass or plastic in which plants are grown
9. do not
10. I am
11. he will/shall
12. we are

13. they have
14. could not
15. knee
16. folk
17. thumb
18. scent
19. design
20. could
21–26. Answers will vary but could include:
noun: book, pen
verb: run, swim
adjective: blue, small
27–30. Answers will vary.

## Paper 10
1. Philip
2. a dog
3. by aeroplane
4. taking care of Scamp while Philip's family are on holiday
5–6. any two of: bed, food bowls, food, lead
7. chase rabbits
8. keep him on his lead
9–14. save, scrap, slipper, smile, snore, storm
15. cat or cot
16. map
17. men
18. pan, pen or pun
19. tin, tan, ton or tun
20. bit, but, bat or bot
21. Is it going to rain later?
22. Where is the park?
23. Your dress is amazing!
24. You must be joking!
25. Who is at the door?
26. Go away!
27. train
28. fair
29. left
30. light

## Paper 11
1. a circus
2. Marco
3. a clown
4. safety net
5. buy 2 adult tickets and get 1 child free
6. Answers will vary.
7. telephone
8. fish
9. funny
10. graph
11. physical
12. faster
13–16. friendly, happy, helpful, sure
Answers will vary but might include:
17. The cat crept silently towards the mouse.
18. Carrie laughed happily when the clown came in.
19. Dad shouted angrily at the naughty puppy.
20. ran
21. brought
22. came
23. wrote

24. read
25. went
26–30. Answers will vary.

## Paper 12
1. this Saturday
2. under 10 years
3. because they wanted a character that both boys and girls would like
4–5. it is pretty fast; it is very high
6–8. Answers will vary.
9. flock
10. herd
11. bunch
12. pack
13. delicious
14. calm
15. interesting
16. blue
17. houses
18. pencils
19. trains
20. books
21. bananas
22. chairs
23. bear
24. peach
25. ear
26. pears
Answers might include:
27. small
28. asleep
29. on
30. new/young

## Paper 13
1. the washing machine
2. the garden fence
3. Spain
4. skidded
5. scrubbing at the paint made the stain bigger
6. Uncle Tom
7–8. the kitchen floor, the hall carpet
9. sadly
10. painful
11. joyful
12. surely
13. bravely
14. playful
15. chemist
16. character
17. chaos
18. choir
19. gather
20. consume
21. doze
22. create
23. scrape
24. discover
25. label
26. muddle
27. model
28. bottle
29. cuddle
30. level

## Paper 14
1. night
2–3. fairy lights, streetlamp
4. it is broken
5. dark clouds
6. shelter
7. rattled, drummed, trickled
8. Answers will vary.
Answers might include:
9–10. hook, book
11–12. told, hold
13–14. hay, grey

2

15–16. stick, lick
Answers may vary:
17. snowman
18. football
19. teapot/teacup
20. bookmark/bookcase
21. ca/mel      22. flow/er
23. sil/ver     24. si/lly
25. un<u>com</u>mon  26. hope<u>less</u>
27. <u>real</u>ly   28. wash<u>able</u>
29. shame<u>ful</u> 30. clear<u>ly</u>

**Paper 15**
1. a play script
2. 3
3. in a town centre
4. shopping
5. puzzled
6. they are organising a surprise birthday party for Caroline
7. Answers might include: delighted
8. Answers will vary.
9. surely       10. gladly
11. quickly     12. strangely
13. gracefully  14. separately
15. stopped     16. purple
17. fourteen    18. people
19. January     20. Thursday
21–26. Answers will vary.
27. peas        28. carrot
29. potatoes    30. onions

**Paper 16**
1. they hear church bells
2. 12
3. toast
4. it is jammed on the rocks
5. the people who sail the ship
6–7. any 2 of: silk, tea sets, spices
8. fishing
9. caught
10. gave
11. fell
12. won
13. I went to the cinema with Rory, Max, Kerry and Matthew.
14. We had fruit, sandwiches, cake and crisps for our picnic.
15. Mum bought pink, yellow, white and red flowers for Gran.
16–20. a, d, e, b, c
21. biggest     22. fitter
23. hottest     24. wetter
25. prettier    26. funniest
27. kennel      28. nest
29. hutch       30. stable

**Paper 17**
1. Dundee
2. she could jump like a flea
3. small insect that can jump very high
4. Answers will vary.
5. she jumped so high she got lost and came down in the sea
6. Answers might include: be
7–8. blue, surprise
9–14. I, October, Robert, London, Spain, Friday
15. gracefully
16. carefully
17. closely
18. messily
19. loudly
20. slowly
21–24. Answers will vary.
25. "You shall go to the ball!" said the fairy godmother.
26. "Can I go to Billy's house?" asked Scott.
27. "Stop tickling me!" giggled Sophie.
28. "It's beautiful!" said Mum, looking at the Christmas tree.
29. "What time is it?" wondered Sam.
30. "Have you finished your work?" asked the teacher.

**Paper 18**
1. 3 or 4
2. so it is fair
3. Answers might include: so they have more pieces to make their towers with
4. Because the team might not have enough sweets left to finish their tower
5. stand up
6. it is the tallest tower that can stand up on its own
7–8. Answers will vary.
9. me          10. she
11. they       12. We
13. us         14. ou
15. ea         16. ie
17. oo         18. oa
19. childhood  20. friendship
21. ownership
22. neighbourhood
23. brotherhood
24. hardship
25–26. Answers will vary.
27. flock      28. shoal
29. swarm      30. gaggle

**Paper 19**
1. locating
2. a dog
3. in the evening
4–5. they were hidden under a ledge; it was dark
6. he barked
7. for a check-up
8. they adopted him from a rescue centre
9. greenhouse
10. blackbird/bluebird
11. bluebell
12. goldfish
13. greyhound
14–18.

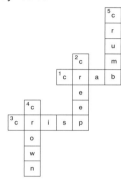

19. April
20. Oscar      21. Liverpool
22. Australia  23. Friday
24. proper nouns are written with a capital letter
25. knot       26. would
27. scene      28. climb
29. talk       30. sign

**Paper 20**
1. a birthday party
2. leave
3. right
4. purple sign
5. five minutes
6. free parking
7. half price parking
8. it is locked from 8.30 p.m.
Answers might include:
9. pretty      10. exciting
11. funny      12. delicious
13. black
14–15. hat, hot, hut, hit
16–17. sit, sat, set
18–19. step, stop
20–21. wish, wash
Answers might include:
22. below      23. hot
24. went       25. soft
26. dry        27. without

Answers might include:

**28.** horse   **29.** badger

**30.** photograph

## Paper 21

**1.** 5
**2.** no
**3.** sandwiches
**4–5.** The soft play area was dirty; the food they ordered took too long to arrive and it wasn't what they ordered.
**6.** it was new
**7.** by making sure that children take their shoes off before they play on the play area
**8.** the play area must be cleaned
**9.** running
**10.** planned
**11.** swimming
**12.** skipped
**13.** hopping
**14.** flapped   **15.** There
**16.** their   **17.** there
**18.** their   **19.** a girl's bag
**20.** the cat's tail
**21.** my dog's nose
**22.** Tom's ball
**23–26.** Answers will vary.
**27.** milk   **28.** rabbit
**29.** pencil   **30.** banana

## Paper 22

**1.** afternoon
**2.** a wall
**3.** because it had been raining heavily the night before
**4.** someone who sees something happen
**5.** to catch up with her family
**6.** the water was moving fast
**7.** slithering
**8.** a lady from a nearby house came out with towels and blankets
**9–10.** rain, roof
**11–12.** water, tea
**13–14.** storm, dream
**15–16.** cough, cream
**17.** brush   **18.** wishes
**19.** apples   **20.** box
**21.** witch   **22.** matches
**23.** badly   **24.** slowly
**25.** properly   **26.** mostly
**27.** I wished it would stop raining.
**28.** We watched TV on Saturday morning.
**29.** Mum and Dad looked angry because of the mess.
**30.** I loved to make models.

## Paper 23

**1.** a king in ancient Egypt
**2.** someone who studies the way people used to live
**3.** a stone box which contains the gold coffin
**4.** beautiful paintings
**5.** they were stolen by thieves
**6.** it had never been found by the thieves
**7.** Howard Carter
**8.** gold
**9.** membership
**10.** boyhood
**11.** motherhood
**12.** partnership
Answers might include:
**13.** box   **14.** climb
**15.** funny   **16.** slowly
**17.** Munday (Monday)
**18.** yelow (yellow)
**19.** Thees (These)
**20.** littel (little)
**21.** meny (many)
**22.** muney (money)
Answers might include:
**23.** rage   **24.** mouse
**25.** steal   **26.** make
**27.** We packed buckets, spades and fishing nets for our trip to the beach.
**28–29.** Gran grows roses, marigolds, daisies and tulips in her garden.
**30.** Ella, Jade and Lucy sit on my table at school.

## Paper 24

**1.** on a farm
**2.** hot
**3.** 12
**4.** he can hardly keep walking
**5–6.** Will's father and his older brother
**7.** because they needed more energy to work hard
**8.** Hay is cut and stored to feed the cows and sheep during the winter, when the grass does not grow.
**9.** prefix   **10.** unable
**11.** renew   **12.** impossible
**13.** misunderstand
**14.** disappoint/reappoint
**15.** signal   **16.** metal
**17.** nibble   **18.** postal
**19.** stable   **20.** middle
**21.** spiteful   **22.** careful
**23.** rudely   **24.** nervously
**25.** cheerful   **26.** boldly
**27.** Grace   **28.** Thursdays
**29.** Africa   **30.** February

4

**Paper 13**

**Level 2**

**6.** Who is going to fix the damage? _Uncle Tom_

**7–8.** In the final paragraph, what two things need to be replaced?

_kitchen floor_  _hall carpet_

Add the **suffix *ful*** or ***ly*** to each of these words.

/8

**9.** sad_ly_

**10.** pain_ful_

**11.** joy_ful_

**12.** sure_ly_

**13.** brave_ly_

**14.** play_ful_

/6

Underline a ***ch*** word in each sentence that begins with a hard ***c*** sound.

**15.** Mum bought medicine from the chemist.

**16.** Goldilocks is my favourite character in the story.

**17.** There was chaos when the spider ran across the floor.

**18.** We listened to the choir singing.

/4

Draw lines to match up **verbs** with a similar meaning.

**19.** collect   scrape

**20.** eat   create

**21.** sleep   gather

**22.** make   discover

**23.** scratch   doze

**24.** find   consume

/6

Add ***le*** or ***el*** to complete each word.

**25.** lab_le_

**26.** mudd_le_

**27.** mod_le_

**28.** bott_el_

**29.** cudd_le_

**30.** lev_el_

/6

/30

35

# Paper 14

## Level 2

## PAPER 14

> Read the description of this setting, then answer the questions.

As night fell, it began to rain. People hurried home, leaving the dark street empty. A broken streetlamp came on, flickered, and went off again. Fairy lights glowed warmly in a shop window and left streaky reflections on the shiny wet pavements. Above, dark clouds hid the moon and stars from view.

In the distance, a train rattled past. Looking for shelter, a stray cat crept down an alleyway. Rain drummed on the street and trickled in little rivers towards the drains.

> Circle your answers.

1. What time of day is described?

   (night)           early morning           lunchtime

2–3. List two types of light that can be seen by the people in the description.

   _street lights_       _fairy lights_

4. Why does the streetlamp go off? _broken_

5. What is hiding the moon and stars from view? _dark clouds_

6. What is the stray cat looking for? _shelter_

7. Find and copy a word that describes a sound that can be heard.

   _drummed_

8. Write a sentence about how this setting makes you feel. Write about what you would want to do if you were in this setting.

   _It makes me feel scared and_
   _I would try to sleep_

/8

36

## Level 2

### Paper 14

**Write two words that rhyme with each word.**

**9–10.** took _shook_ _hook_

**11–12.** bold _hold_ _cold_

**13–14.** say _may_ _lay_

**15–16.** brick _trick_ _drick_ /8

**Add a second word to each of these, to make a compound word.**

**17.** snow _storm_ **18.** foot _feet_

**19.** tea _____ **20.** book _song_ /4

**Draw a line to split each word into two syllables.**

**21.** camel **22.** flower **23.** silver **24.** silly /4

**Underline the root word in each word.**

**25.** uncommon **26.** hopeless

**27.** really **28.** washable

**29.** shameful **30.** clearly /6

/30

# PAPER 15

**A special secret**

[Two friends, Amy and Beth, are shopping in town when they bump into another friend, Caroline.]

Caroline: Hi Amy, hi Beth.

Amy: [looks a bit embarrassed] Hi Caroline. We are just, um, shopping.

Caroline: Have you bought anything good?

Beth: No! Nothing at all. We must go. See you on Monday.

[Amy and Beth hurry away, leaving Caroline looking puzzled.]

Caroline: [to herself] I hope I haven't done anything to upset them. I thought we didn't have any secrets from each other.

[Caroline walks off in the opposite direction. Amy and Beth come back.]

Amy: Do you think she guessed our secret?

Beth: No, I don't think so.

Amy: Good. Her surprise birthday party will be the best ever!

**Circle your answers.**

**1.** What kind of text is this?

(a play script)　　　　a letter　　　　a newspaper report

**2.** How many characters are involved in the text?

1　　　　2　　　　(3)

**3.** Where is the scene set?

in a school　　　　in a cinema　　　　(in a town centre)

**Answer the questions.**

**4.** What does Amy tell Caroline she and Beth are doing? _Shopping_

**Level 2**

**Paper 15**

**5.** Find and copy the word that describes how Caroline feels about the behaviour of Amy and Beth.

_puzzeld_

**6.** What is the special secret that Amy and Beth are trying to hide?

_birthday suprise_

**7.** Think of a word to describe how you think Caroline will feel when she knows what her friends are planning.

_suprised_

**8.** Write a sentence about a time when you have planned something exciting for someone else.

_Mum's birthday party._

/8

Add *ly* to each word to make an **adverb**.

**9.** sure + ly = _surely_

**10.** glad + ly = ~~glarely~~ _gladly_

**11.** quick + ly = _quickly_

**12.** strange + ly = _strangely_

**13.** graceful + ly = _gracefeul_

**14.** separate + ly = _separate_

/6

Underline the correctly spelled word in each pair.

**15.** stopped — stoped

**16.** purpel — purple

**17.** foreteen — fourteen

**18.** peeple — people

**19.** January — Janury

**20.** Thersday — Thursday

/6

# Paper 15

## Level 2

Use the bold **wh** words to help you complete each sentence in a really interesting way.

21. **When** I am grown up I would like to be ___scientice___.

22. I would love to know **why** ~~____~~ people smoke.

23. I wonder **where** I can see ___a real sienctise___.

24. I would love to have a friend **who** ___is one___.

25. I wish I knew **what** would happen next ___year___.

26. **Whenever** there is a thunderstorm I want to ___hid under a___ ~~peey~~ pillow.

/6

Add the missing **consonants** to complete the names of the vegetables in each picture.

27.   p ea s

28.   c a r r o t

29.   p o t a t oe s

30.   o n i o n s

/4

/30

Level 2

Paper 16

# PAPER 16

It was early morning when we heard the church bells ringing. It wasn't Sunday, so we knew there wasn't a church service. There was only one thing it could be. A shipwreck!

Pulling on his boots, Dad grabbed some toast and dashed out of the door. I wanted to follow but I knew Mum wouldn't let me go until I had finished my porridge.

By the time we got down to the shore, we could see the wreck, jammed on the rocks off Tinker's Point. Dozens of little fishing boats were heading towards it in the sea. I knew Dad's boat would be out there somewhere, but I couldn't see it.

Boats were wrecked on those rocks every year. I knew the ship would not sink for now. It would be stuck on the rocks until the tide washed it free later in the day. There was always plenty of time to rescue the crew.

The barrels and crates the ship was carrying were another matter. Once the men from the ship were safely ashore, anyone with a little boat would be back in the water again, fishing for crates of colourful silk, fancy tea sets or spices from far away.

Circle your answers.

**1.** How do the villagers know there has been a shipwreck?

it is breakfast time    they hear church bells    (it isn't Sunday)

**2.** The text talks about *dozens of small fishing boats*. How many is a dozen?

(12)    10    20

**3.** What does the child's Dad take with him to eat when he leaves the house?

porridge    tea    (toast)

Answer these questions.

**4.** Why isn't the ship sinking straight away?

Because there was a ship wreck.

# Paper 16

## Level 2

**5.** What does the word *crew* mean?

_group_

**6–7.** Name two things that might be washed up from the shipwreck.

_barrels_          _carbes_

**8.** What are the little boats in the story normally used for?

_fishing, getting spices_

/8

> Circle the correct **past tense verb**.

**9.** catch          catched          (caught)

**10.** give          (gave)          gived

**11.** fall          (fell)          falled

**12.** win          winned          (won)

/4

> Write these sentences again, with the **commas** in the correct place.

**13.** I went to the cinema with Rory, Max Kerry, and Matthew.

_I went to the cinema with Rory, Max, Kerry and Mattew._

**14.** We, had fruit sandwiches cake and crisps for our picnic.

_We had fruit, sandwitcles calce and crisps for our picnic._

**15.** Mum bought pink yellow, white and red, flowers for Gran.

_Mum baught pink, yellow, white, and red flowers for Grran._

/3

42

Paper
16

Level 2

**16–20.** Use the bold time words to help you put these sentences in order.
Label them a–e to show the correct order.

(a) When we decided to build a pond, the **first** thing we did was to dig a hole.

(d) **After** the liner was in place, we filled it with water.

(e) **Finally**, we added pond plants.

(b) **Second**, we took out any sharp stones.

(c) **When** the hole was smooth, we put in a pond liner.

/5

Add the missing **adjectives** to the chart.

| | | add er | add est |
|---|---|---|---|
| **21.** | big | bigger | biggest |
| **22.** | fit | fitter | fittest |
| **23.** | hot | hotter | hottest |
| **24.** | wet | wotter | wettest |
| **25.** | pretty | pretter | prettiest |
| **26.** | funny | funnier | funnest |

/6

Draw lines to match each word to the correct **definition**.

**27.** A small hut for a dog to live in.        stable

**28.** A collection of twigs and moss that a
bird lays its eggs in.        hutch

**29.** The special cage a pet rabbit lives in.        kennel

**30.** The building a horse or pony lives in.        nest

/4

/30

# Paper 17

## Level 2

### PAPER 17

There once was a girl from Dundee
Who found she could jump like a flea.
She once jumped so high
She got lost in the sky
And came down on a boat out at sea.

1. Where did the girl in the poem come from? _Dundee_

2. What special skill did she have? _jump like a flea._

3. What is a *flea*? _a bug._

4. Can you think of another animal that is good at jumping? _rabbit_

5. How did the girl end up on a boat out at sea? _because she got lost ~~ing~~ in the sea._

6. In the poem, the words Dundee, flea and sea all **rhyme**. Write another word that rhymes with them. _me_

7–8. Now circle the best words from the brackets to complete this poem. Remember to pick words that rhyme with the final bold word in the line before.

There was a young boy called **Andrew**,
Who dreamed that the whole world was [red (blue)].
He opened his **eyes**
And to his [(surprise) anger]
He found out that it was quite true!

/8

9–14. Circle the words that should always begin with a capital letter.

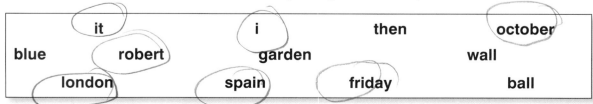

/6

**Paper 17**

**Level 2**

Underline the **adverb** in each sentence.

15. The ballerinas danced gracefully.

16. We crossed the road carefully.

17. Dad looked closely at my school report.

18. Babies often eat messily.

19. An owl hooted loudly in the trees.

20. The tide slowly washed our sandcastle away.

/6

21–24. Write simple instructions for playing your favourite playground game.

• Hopscotch
• draw a box then two and 1 and so on
• add numbers and play.

/4

Put **speech marks** around the words that someone has said.

25. "You shall go to the ball!" said the fairy godmother.

26. "Can I go to Billy's house?" asked Scott.

27. "Stop tickling me!" giggled Sophie.

28. "It's beautiful!" said Mum, looking at the Christmas tree.

29. "What time is it?" wondered Sam.

/6

30. "Have you finished your work?" asked the teacher.

/30

Paper
18

Level 2

## PAPER 18

**Pasta Towers**

Pasta Towers is a game you play in teams of three or four people. The aim of the game is to build towers using only dried spaghetti and jelly sweets. The winning team is the one with the highest tower.

1. Give each team 15 jelly sweets and 20 pieces of dried spaghetti.
2. Set a timer to time 20 minutes. This is how long the teams have to build their towers.
3. Teams can break the jelly sweets or spaghetti into smaller pieces if they want to.
4. Teams can eat the jelly sweets if they want to, but they may not have enough left to finish their tower!
5. The finished towers must be able to stand up on their own.

Circle your answer.

**1.** How many people should each team have?

1 or 2                 2 or 3                 3 or 4

Answer these questions.

**2.** Why do you think each team should begin with the same amount of sweets and pasta? _Otherwise it's not fair_

**3.** Suggest one reason why some teams decide to break the sweets or pasta up into smaller pieces? _to have more pieces._

**4.** Sweets are tasty, but why might it be a bad idea to eat the sweets?
_might not have enough ~~fot~~ for tow_

**5.** What must the towers be able to do on their own? _stand_

**6.** How is the winning tower chosen? _tallest tower._

46

**Paper 18**

**Level 2**

**7–8.** Imagine you were leading a team in this game. Write two sentences outlining your ideas for how your team could win the competition. Remember to give reasons for both of your ideas.

_____

_____

_____

/8

Underline the **personal pronoun** in each sentence.

**9.** Jacob invited me to the party.

**10.** Mum was in a hurry because she was late for work.

**11.** The boys were excited because they won the football match.

**12.** We are going to Spain on holiday.

**13.** Gran bought us tickets for the show.

/5

Write the **vowel** pattern that the words in each group share.

| | | | | |
|---|---|---|---|---|
| **14.** flour | your | cloud | youth | _ou_ |
| **15.** heart | ear | pear | sweat | _ea_ |
| **16.** pie | piece | thief | cried | _ie_ |
| **17.** food | floor | hook | room | _oo_ |
| **18.** boat | roar | roam | groan | _oa_ |

/5

# Paper 18

## Level 2

Add the **suffix *ship*** or ***hood*** to complete each word.

**19.** child + _hood_ = _childhood_

**20.** friend + _ship_ = _friendship_

**21.** owner + _ship_ = _ownership_

**22.** neighbour + _hood_ = _nieghbourhood_

**23.** brother + _hood_ = _brotherhood_

**24.** hard + _ship_ = _hardship_ /6

Think of interesting ways to complete these questions. Remember the **question mark**!

**25.** How old _are you?_

**26.** Where are _you?_ /2

Underline the **collective noun** in each sentence.

**27.** A flock of seagulls flew out to sea.

**28.** We saw a shoal of fish in the shallow water.

**29.** They ran from the swarm of bees.

**30.** A gaggle of geese waddled across the farmyard. /4

/30

Paper

19

Level 2

## PAPER 19

**Barley saves the day**

A family pet is being hailed a hero this week after locating two missing boys stranded on the cliff above Parley Point. Heroic hound Barley found the boys stranded on the cliff then barked for half an hour to attract the attention of rescue workers searching nearby.

Mary Connor is the mother of Ian Connor, one of the missing boys. She explains: "It was late and starting to get dark, so it was very difficult to see anything but then Barley started barking. He just wouldn't stop and in the end, we realised he must have found the boys. They were hidden under a ledge of rock, so we couldn't see them in the dark, but somehow he knew they were there."

Ian and his friend Usman were taken to hospital for a check-up but allowed home later in the evening. Both are doing well and hope to be back at school soon.

Ian says: "We got Barley from a dog rescue centre because his old owner didn't want him any more. I think that helping us was his way of saying thank you. He is the best dog ever."

Circle your answers.

**1.** What word in the first sentence has a similar meaning to the word *finding*?

locating        hailed        stranded

**2.** What kind of animal is Barley?

a horse        a dog        a cat

**3.** What time of day did the rescue take place?

in the morning        in the evening        at lunchtime

Answer these questions.

**4–5.** Write two reasons why it was difficult for the rescuers to see the boys on the cliff.

*dark and a rock was covering them*

49

# Paper 19

## Level 2

**6.** How did the rescuers know that Barley had found the boys?

He did not stop shouting.

**7.** Why were the boys taken to the hospital after they were rescued?

cheacke up

**8.** Ian says that Barley may have helped them as his way of saying thank you. According to the story, what might Barley want to thank the family for?

because they got him from dog centre.

/8

Add a colour from the box to each word to make a **compound word**.

| black | blue | gold | green | grey |

**9.** green house

**10.** blue bird

**11.** black bell

**12.** gold fish

**13.** grey hound

/5

**Paper 19**

## Level 2

**14–18.** Label these words 1–5 to put them in alphabetical order and then fit them into the crossword grid.

4 — crown   1 — crab   3 — crisp   2 — creep   5 — crumb

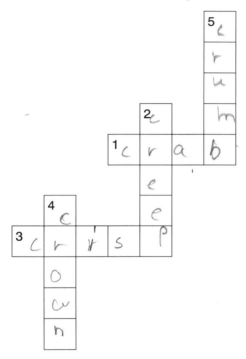

/5

> Underline a **proper noun** in each sentence.

19. We moved house last April.

20. Our cat is called Oscar.

21. I visited my friends in Liverpool.

22. There are kangaroos in Australia.

23. There is a school trip on Friday.

/5

24. What is special about the way we write proper nouns?

_____

/1

# Paper 20

## Level 2

Add the missing silent letters to these words.

**25.** _k_not

**26.** wou_l_d

**27.** s_c_ene

**28.** clim_b_

**29.** ta_l_k

**30.** si_g_n

/6

/30

## PAPER 20

Thank you for booking your birthday party at CJ Bowling. We are easy to find and just five minutes from the motorway!

Just exit the motorway (M4) at junction 12 and follow the signs for the Town Centre. At the traffic lights, turn right and continue until you reach the large roundabout by the theatre. Turn left at this roundabout and continue for about a mile. Just after the park, you will come to another set of traffic lights. Carry on straight through the lights then take the second turning on the left, into Harris Street. Look out for the purple CJ Bowling Car Park sign, on the right. Remember, parking is free for the family of the birthday boy or girl and half price for all guests at our bowling parties!

Car park full? Alternative parking is available in the Orchards Shopping Centre car park. (If you are attending an evening party, please be aware that this car park is locked from 8.30 p.m.).

Circle your answers.

**1.** What has been booked at CJ Bowling?

a birthday party          a competition          a family bowling game

**2.** What does the word *exit* mean in the third sentence?

follow          leave          drive

Paper
20

Level 2

**3.** Which direction should you take at the first set of traffic lights you come to?

straight on                 left                 right

**4.** What will drivers see that tells them they have found CJ Bowling's car park?

_____ sign _____

**5.** How long is the journey likely to take from leaving the motorway?

5 min

**6–7.** Describe two different parking price offers available to customers going to a bowling party.

family of the birthday boy or girl _____ free _____

guests at the party _____ half price _____

**8.** The directions suggest another car park customers can use if the CJ Bowling Car Park is full. Why might it be a bad idea to use it if you are going to an evening party?

_____ eart car park closes at 8:30pm _____

/8

Add a suitable **adjective** to complete each sentence.

**9.** Chloe chose a _____ nice _____ dress for the party.

**10.** The football match was _____ amazing _____.

**11.** The circus clown was _____ funny _____.

**12.** I chose a _____ ice _____ cream cake at the bakers.

**13.** A _____ chicken _____ beetle ran across the floor.

/5

Add different **vowels** to complete these pairs of words.

**14–15.** h_a_t          h_i_t          **16–17.** s_i_t          s_a_t

**18–19.** st_o_p          st_a_p          **20–21.** w_i_sh          w_a_sh

/8

# Paper 21

## Level 2

### Write **antonyms** for these words.

**22.** above _____  **23.** cold _____

**24.** came _____  **25.** hard _____

**26.** wet _____  **27.** with _____  /6

### Write words with the correct number of **syllables**.

**28.** 1 syllable _____

**29.** 2 syllables _____  /3

**30.** 3 syllables _____

/30

## PAPER 21

Dear Mr Daye,

I am writing to complain about our visit to Happy Daye's Activity Land earlier this week. I brought my three children to the centre along with two of their friends because we have always enjoyed our visits before. However, on this occasion our experience was very different.

To begin with, the soft play area was filthy and very slippery because some children had been allowed to play on it wearing wet shoes. My daughter's new white top is now covered in stains that will not wash out. The sandwiches we ordered in the cafe took 40 minutes to arrive and when they did finally come, they were not what we had ordered.

Happy Daye's always used to be great, but we will not be visiting again until the soft play area has been cleaned.

Yours sincerely,

Mrs Mandy Hart

## Paper 21

### Level 2

**Circle your answers.**

**1.** How many children did Mrs Hart take to Happy Daye's Activity Land?

2                  3                  5

**2.** Did the group enjoy their latest visit?

yes            no            the letter doesn't say

**3.** What did they order in the café?

cakes           sandwiches           nothing

**Answer these questions.**

**4–5.** Find and describe two things that Mrs Hart is complaining about in the letter.

_____

_____

**6.** Why do you think Mrs Hart is particularly cross about the damage to her daughter's top? _____

**7.** How could the problems on the soft play area have been prevented?

_____

**8.** What does Mrs Hart say must happen before she would take her children to Happy Daye's again? _____    /8

**Complete these word sums, changing the spelling where necessary.**

**9.** run + ing   = _____

**10.** plan + ed   = _____

**11.** swim + ing = _____

**12.** skip + ed   = _____

**13.** hop + ing   = _____    /6

**14.** flap + ed   = _____

55

# Paper 21

## Level 2

**Underline the correct word to complete each sentence.**

**15.** (Their  There) is a circus in the park.

**16.** The boys ate (their  there) packed lunches quickly.

**17.** "Is (there  their) any cake left?" asked Max.

**18.** Kate and Marcia took (there  their) coats because it was cold.  /4

**Add the possessive apostrophe to each phrase.**

**19.** a girls bag

**20.** the cats tail

**21.** my dogs nose

**22.** Toms ball  /4

**Write an interesting sentence using each of these adverbs.**

**23.** bravely _____

**24.** rudely _____

**25.** brightly _____

**26.** carefully _____

/4

**Write the best word for each definition.**

**27.** A white liquid often used as a drink or poured over breakfast cereal.

_____

**28.** A small furry animal with long ears that is often kept as a pet.

_____

**29.** A long thin object used for writing that is often made of wood.  /4

_____

**30.** A long, curved yellow fruit. _____

/30

# PAPER 22

**Witness report**

I was walking along Brook Lane at about 4.30 p.m. on Thursday. A young girl was ahead of me, walking with her family. I saw her climb onto the wall that separates the pavement from the river. She walked carefully along the wall for a while but her family was walking more quickly and she started to fall behind. She started to walk more quickly and then to run along the wall.

Suddenly she slipped off the wall and fell into the river. The water was quite deep that day because it had been raining heavily the night before. The girl could stand on the bottom of the river but the water came up to her waist and she kept being swept along by the fast-moving water.

She grabbed hold of a tree that was growing out from the bank and I could see her holding on tightly. By this time, her father had run back along the pavement and was slithering down the bank of the river towards her. He grabbed hold of her and helped her back up the steep bank to the pavement. A lady came out of a nearby house with towels and blankets for the girl and her father, who were both wet and cold.

**Circle your answers.**

**1.** What time of day did the incident happen?

morning afternoon evening

**2.** What was the girl walking along when she slipped into the water?

a wall a fence a pavement

**3.** Why was the water quite deep that day?

because it came up to her waist

because it was Thursday

because it had been raining heavily the night before

**Paper 22**

**Level 2**

> Answer these questions.

**4.** This is a witness report that describes what someone saw.
What do you think a *witness* is?

_____

**5.** The witness says that the accident happened after the girl began to hurry
along the wall. Why do you think she did this?

_____

**6.** Although the girl could stand up in the river, she kept being swept along.
Why was this?

_____

**7.** Find and copy a word that describes how the girl's father climbed down the
steep river bank.

_____

**8.** Who else helped the girl, after she had been rescued from the river, and how?

_____

/8

> Complete both words in each pair by adding a **consonant** from the box.
> Use the same letter for the words in each pair.

| t | c | r | m |
|---|---|---|---|

**9–10.** _____ain    _____oof          **11–12.** wa_____er  _____ea

**13–14.** stor_____    drea_____          **15–16.** _____ough  _____ream

/8

58

# Paper 22

**Level 2**

Complete the table of **singular** and **plural nouns**.

|     | singular | plural  |
|-----|----------|---------|
| 17. |          | brushes |
| 18. | wish     |         |
| 19. | apple    |         |
| 20. |          | boxes   |
| 21. |          | witches |
| 22. | match    |         |

/6

Add the **suffix ly** to turn these words into **adverbs**.

23. bad          _____        24. slow          _____

25. proper       _____        26. most          _____

/4

Write these sentences again changing the bold **verb** to the **past tense**.

27. I **wish** it would stop raining.

    _____

28. We **watch** TV on Saturday morning.

    _____

29. Mum and Dad **look** angry because of the mess.

    _____

30. I **love** to make models.

    _____

/4

/30

# PAPER 23

**The tomb of Tutankhamun**

Many people are fascinated by ancient Egypt and often the most interesting things are the beautiful tombs and temples the Egyptians built. One of the most famous tombs belongs to Tutankhamun. He was only eight or nine years old when he ruled Egypt and he died when he was just 19 years old. Like many other pharaohs, he was buried in a tomb in the Valley of the Kings in Egypt.

Most of the tombs in the Valley of the Kings are empty except for beautifully painted walls, because thousands of years ago, thieves stole the treasures they contained. What is so special about Tutankhamun's tomb is that it was never found by thieves. Instead, it was discovered in 1922 by an archaeologist called Howard Carter. When he opened the tomb, he was the first person to have seen inside since it was sealed up after Tutankhamun's death. Inside, the tomb was filled with beautiful gold furniture, chariots and statues, as well as the pharaoh's stone sarcophagus, which contained his gold coffin.

The riches found have become world famous and some of the objects from the tomb have been displayed in museums around the world. However, archaeologists believe that some of the other tombs in the valley would originally have contained even more beautiful and valuable things. These have been stolen over the years and have disappeared. Just imagine what they would have looked like!

Draw lines to match each word with the correct **definition**.

**1.** pharaoh      a stone box which contains the gold coffin

**2.** archaeologist    a king in ancient Egypt

**3.** sarcophagus    someone who studies the way people used to live

Answer these questions.

**4.** What is on the walls of many of the tombs in the Valley of the Kings?

_____

Paper
**23**

Level 2

**5.** What happened to the treasures buried in many of the tombs?

_____

**6.** Why were there still treasures in the tomb of Tutankhamun when it was found in 1922? _____

**7.** Who discovered the tomb? _____

**8.** Which valuable metal was used to make many of the treasures in the tomb?

_____

/8

Write each word again, adding the **suffix *ship*** or ***hood***.

**9.** member _____

**10.** boy _____

**11.** mother _____

**12.** partner _____

/4

Write an example of each type of word.

**13.** noun _____

**14.** verb _____

**15.** adjective _____

**16.** adverb _____

/4

Underline a word in each sentence that is spelled incorrectly.

**17.** We are going skating on Munday.

**18.** There are big yelow sunflowers in our garden.

**19.** Thees shoes are too small for me.

**20.** A littel girl played in the park.

**21.** How meny children are coming to the party?

/6

**22.** Alice spent her pocket muney on comics.

61

# Paper 24

## Level 3

Write a word that **rhymes** with each of these words.

**23.** cage   _____

**24.** house   _____

**25.** real   _____

**26.** snake   _____

/4

Add **commas** to these sentences.

**27.** We packed buckets spades and fishing nets for our trip to the beach.

**28–29.** Gran grows roses marigolds daisies and tulips in her garden.

**30.** Ella Jade and Lucy sit on my table at school.

/4

/30

## PAPER 24

By the time Will got home from the farm, he was starving hungry and so tired he could barely keep walking. There was never enough food to go around and Will was used to going to bed hungry. He knew it would be different today, though. Now he was working, like his father and older brother, he knew he would get a bigger share of whatever food there was. He would need it too.

His first day at the farm had been very hard. He had spent twelve hours in the hot sun, tying hay into bales. They would be used to feed the cows and sheep in the winter, when the frost stopped the grass from growing. Will wondered what his family would be eating that winter. Nothing much grew during the coldest months of the year, just when you needed the extra food to help keep you warm. He shivered, just thinking about it.

Level 3

**Paper 24**

> Circle your answers.

**1.** Where does Will work?

on a farm                    in a factory                    at home

**2.** What had the weather been like that day?

cold                    wet                    hot

**3.** How many hours had Will worked that day?

2                    12                    the text does not say

**4.** How do we know that Will is very tired when he gets home?

_____

**5–6.** Apart from Will, who else in the story goes out to work?

_____        _____

**7.** Why do you think that people who worked would have needed to eat more?

_____

**8.** Explain in your own words why the farm that Will works on cuts and stores hay.

_____

_____

/8

> Pick a **prefix** from the box to add to each word.

| im | un | re | mis |
|----|----|----|-----|
|    | dis | pre |    |

**9.** ____fix          **10.** ____able          **11.** ____new

**12.** ____possible    **13.** ____understand    **14.** ____appoint

/6

63

**Paper 24**

## Level 3

Circle the correctly spelled word in each group.

**15.** signal      signel      signle

**16.** metle      metal      metel

**17.** nibbel      nibbal      nibble

**18.** postel      postal      postle

**19.** stabel      stable      stabal

**20.** middal      middel      middle

/6

Add the **suffix *ly*** or ***ful*** to each word.

**21.** spite____      **22.** care____      **23.** rude____

**24.** nervous____      **25.** cheer____      **26.** bold____

/6

Write these sentences again, using a capital letter for the **proper nouns**.

**27.** My friend grace loves gymnastics.

_____

**28.** On thursdays we have swimming at school.

_____

**29.** There are lions in africa.

_____

**30.** It is often very cold in february.

/4

_____

/30

# Glossary

| | |
|---|---|
| **adjective** | a word that describes a **noun**, e.g. tiny, green |
| **adverb** | a word that describes a **verb**, e.g. kindly, prettily |
| **alphabetical order** | the order of the letters in the alphabet |
| **antonym** | a word with the opposite meaning to another word, e.g. tall, short |
| **apostrophe** | a **punctuation mark** used to show possession or **contraction** |
| **blurb** | a short description about a book, usually found on the back cover of the book |
| **collective noun** | a way of describing a group of a particular thing, e.g. flock of sheep |
| **comma** | a **punctuation mark** used to indicate a pause in a sentence, or separate items in a list |
| **compound word** | a word made up of two other words, e.g. footpath |
| **consonant** | the letters of the alphabet that are not **vowels** |
| **contraction** | two words joined together, where an **apostrophe** marks letters that have been removed, e.g. do not = don't |
| **definition** | the meaning of a word |
| **exclamation mark** | a **punctuation mark** used at the end of sentences to show surprise or deliver an order, e.g. Stop! |
| **homophone** | a word which sounds the same but has a different spelling, e.g. maid, made |
| **noun** | a word that names a thing or person |
| **past tense** | a **verb** that describes something that has already happened |
| **personal pronoun** | a **pronoun** used to replace the names of people, e.g. she, me, him |
| **plural** | more than one of something |
| **prefix** | a group of letters added to the beginning of a word to alter its meaning, e.g. *re, ex, co* |
| **present tense** | a **verb** that describes what is happening now |
| **pronoun** | a word that can be used in the place of a **noun** |
| **proper noun** | the name of a person, place, day of the week, month of the year etc, e.g. Jill, March, Rome |
| **question mark** | a **punctuation mark** used at the end of sentences that ask a question, e.g. who? |

## Glossary

| | |
|---|---|
| **rhyme** | the ending of words that sound the same, e.g. bag, flag |
| **root word** | a word that **prefixes** or **suffixes** can be added to, to make new words |
| **singular** | just one of something |
| **speech mark** | **punctuation marks** used at the start and the end of the actual words that a character says, e.g. "Hi" |
| **suffix** | a group of letters added to the end of a word to alter its meaning, e.g. *less*, *ful*, *ly* |
| **syllables** | the beats in a word |
| **synonym** | a word with a similar meaning to another word, e.g. large, huge |
| **verb** | a doing or being word |
| **vowel** | the letters of the alphabet *a*, *e*, *i*, *o* and *u* |

# Progress grid

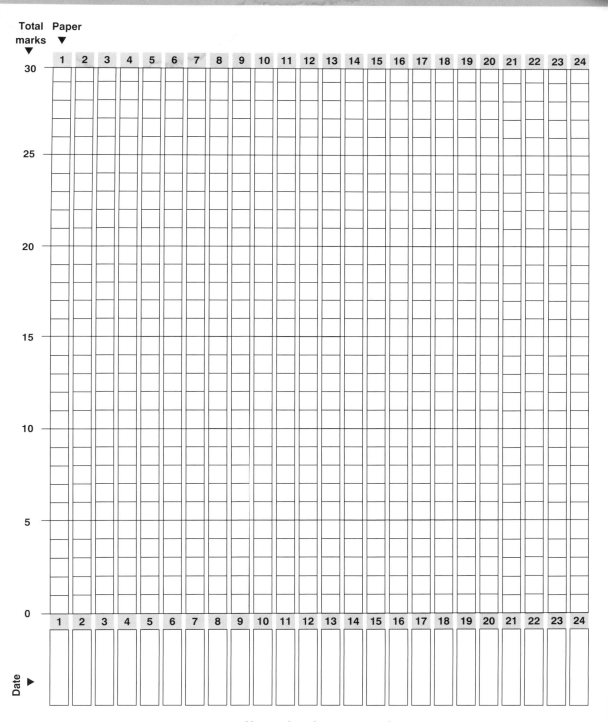

Now colour in your score!

# Notes

# 'Twixt Bay & Burn'

A History of Helen's Bay & Crawfordsburn

*Bayburn Historical Society*

# Contents

Foreword     3

## Chapter 1 – The Beginnings

Introduction     4
Geology and Pre-History     4
Sixteenth and Seventeenth Centuries     7
Maps, Rent Rolls and Other Sources     9
The Ballydavey Massacre –
26 January 1642     17
The Old Inn, Crawfordsburn     19

## Chapter 2 – The Development of Helen's Bay and Crawfordsburn

The Clandeboye Contribution     25
The Belfast and County Down Railway –
'Every Creeping Thing'     31
Other Forms of Transport     34

## Chapter 3 – Farming and Business Life in Former Times

The Rural Scene     37
In the Two Villages     46

## Chapter 4 – Schools

Schools in the Two Villages     52
Nearby Schools     55
Sunday Schools and Other
Children's Organisations     58

## Chapter 5 – Growing up in Crawfordsburn and Helen's Bay

A Range of Reminiscences     61

## Chapter 6 – The Churches

The Beginnings – the Presbyterian Church
at Ballygilbert     72
Helen's Bay Presbyterian Church     73
Church of St John Baptist, Helen's Bay     78

## Chapter 7 – In the Wars

Grey Point Fort     83
Recollections of Colonel Bertram Cotton     88
Wartime Recollections of Jim Page     91
The Home Front including Helen's Bay
Home Guard and Volunteers in
Crawfordsburn     91
My Wartime Memories by
Kathleen Davis     95
The POW Camp at Rockport     96

## Chapter 8 – The Social Fabric

The Bayburn Historical Society     99
Fifty Years of Brownies in the Bay     99
Crawfordsburn Country Club     100
Helen's Bay Golf Club     105
Helen's Bay Lawn Tennis Club     107
Crawfordsburn and Helen's Bay –
Masonic Order     108
Crawfordsburn and Helen's Bay –
Orange Lodge     109
Helen's Bay Players     109
Helen's Bay Police Station     111
The Royal British Legion     112
Scout Camp at Crawfordsburn
Country Park     114
St John's Badminton Club     115
Yachting     116

## Chapter 9 – The Sharman Crawfords of Crawfordsburn House

William Sharman Crawford     118
The Sharman Crawford Children     122
The later Sharman Crawfords     123

## Chapter 10 – Personal Perspectives and other Notables

The Brown Family – a Glance into
the Past     128
Down our Way by 'Rene Shuttleworth     129
Helen's Bay Remembered by Jim Page     131
Craigdarragh House – Workman Family     133
Sir Crawford McCullagh of Rust Hall     134
Coastguards and Customs     134
George Best in Helen's Bay     136

## Chapter 11 – The Ratepayers Association

Local History from the Minutes of
the Association     137

## Chapter 12 – Natural History and Other Aspects of Local Interest

Crawfordsburn Country Park     144
Flora and Fauna     146
The Butterflies of Helen's Bay
and Crawfordsburn     146
The Crawfordsburn Fern     147
Local Weather     148

## Bibliography and Further Reading     150

## Acknowledgements     151